Love from Katy

by Jacqueline Wilson

HAYGROVE SCHOOL
LEARNING SUPPORT
ON LOAN

Illustrated by Connie Jude

Introduction

Katy sees Dave on the bus every morning.
She thinks he's wonderful. Dave doesn't even
seem to notice Katy.

Katy's too shy to try to talk to Dave.
She writes him letters instead, putting down her secret thoughts.
She doesn't dream of sending the letters.
She keeps them safe in her school bag.
But one day ... the letters go missing!

The Letters

Dear Dave

You don't know me.
But I know you.
I know a lot about you. I know your name is David Robinson because I've seen it written on your school bag. I like your writing. It's big and bold.

My writing's little and squiggly. I've written all over my notebook and my pencil case and inside my desk. I've written your name. David Robinson, David Robinson, David Robinson.

Hundreds of little squiggly David Robinsons.

I expect the teachers at your school call you David. And maybe your mum and dad. But all your mates call you Dave. I've heard them on the bus.

So I'll call you Dave too. Is that OK?

Love from
Katy
XXX

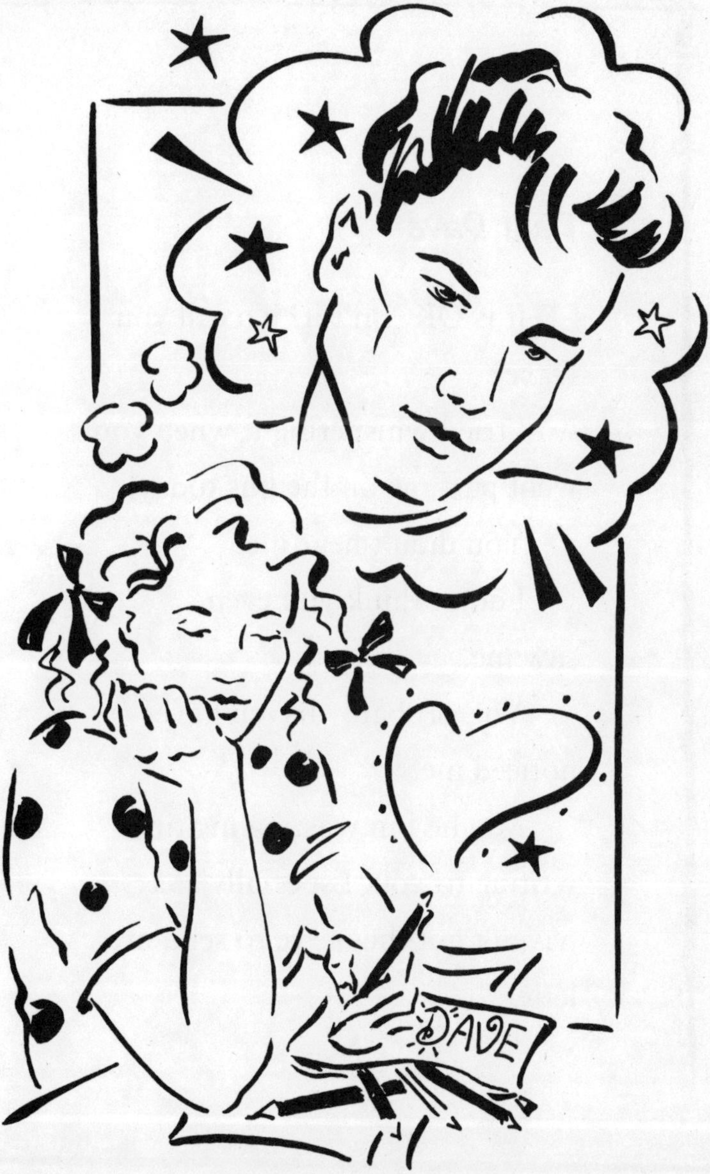
DAVE

Dear Dave

It is OK, isn't it? To call you Dave?

I tried whispering it when you went past me on the bus today.

You didn't hear me.

I don't think you even saw me.

You probably haven't ever noticed me.

Maybe I'm wasting my time writing to you. Especially as I haven't got the nerve to send my letters.

My friend Sarah says I'm
nuts.
Yes, I *am* nuts.
Nuts about you.

Love from
Katy
xxx

Dear Dave

You don't mind me writing to you, do you?

Well, you don't know that I *am* writing, so I suppose that's a daft question.

I do like writing to you. It's funny, because I usually hate writing letters. I can never think what to say.

But there's lots and lots and lots I want to say to you, Dave.

Love from
Katy
XXX

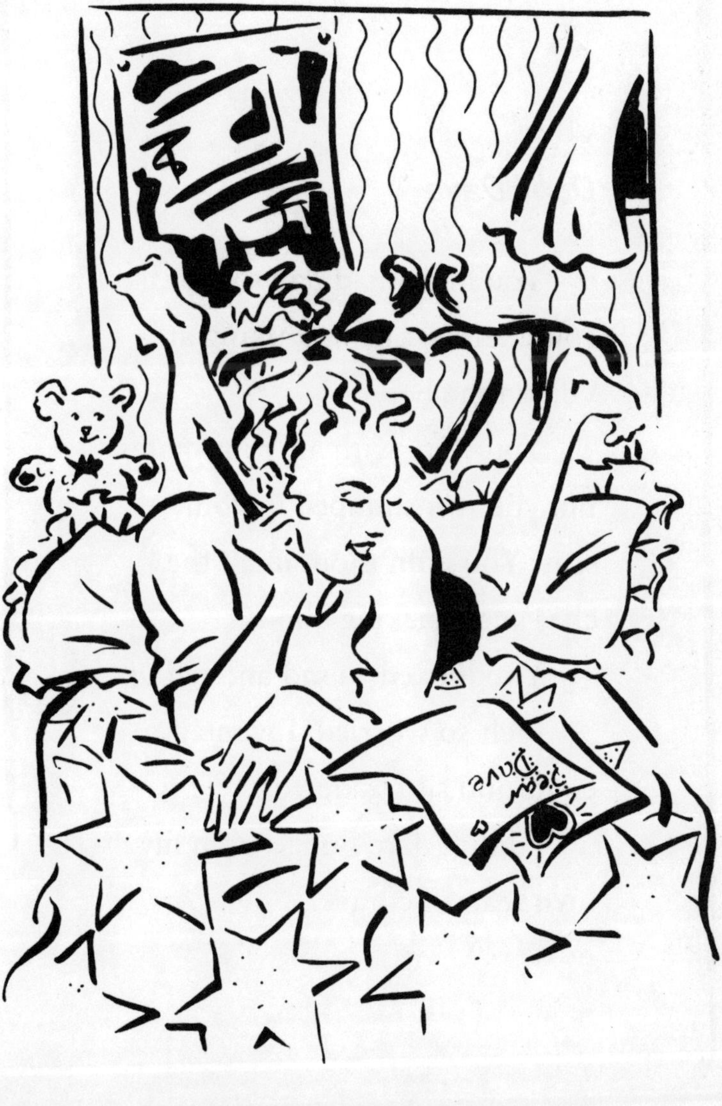
Dear Dave

Dear Dave

You had a bad day today. I could tell just from looking at you on the bus.

You were with all your mates but you just slumped in your seat. You didn't join in all the chat and mucking about.

You looked so sad and fed up.

I felt so worried. I wanted to come and sit beside you.

I didn't dare budge from my own seat, of course.

I sat there and stared at you, trying to send little loving messages to you.

My poor darling Dave, what's up?

**Love from
Katy
xxx**

Dear Dave

You still looked fed up today. And you didn't sleep well, did you? The back of your hair was sticking up as if you'd been tossing and turning all night long.

I do like your hair, even when it's sticking up. And your eyes. And your mouth. You've got such a lovely smile.

Only you still weren't smiling today.

I tried smiling at you when I got off the bus at my stop. Well, I was going to smile but I felt so shy and stupid that I turned my head away at the last moment.

**Love from
Katy
XXX**

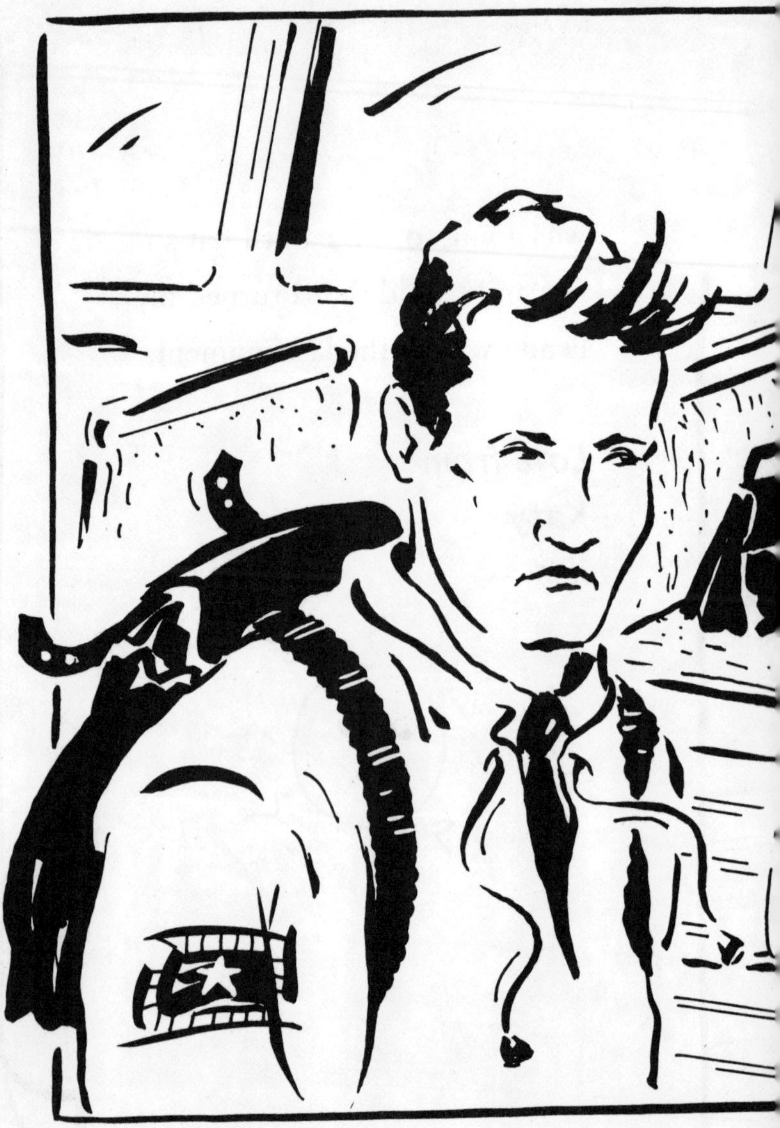

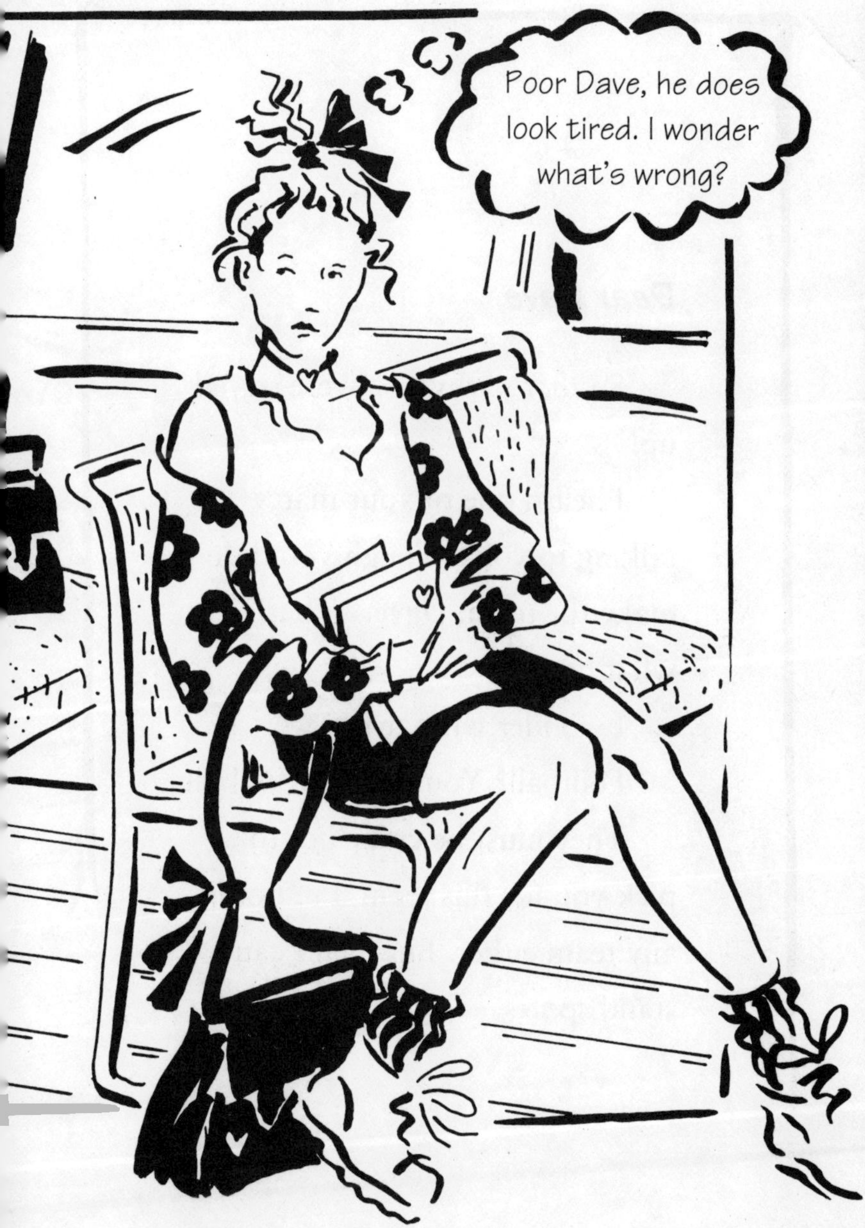
Poor Dave, he does look tired. I wonder what's wrong?

Dear Dave

So *that's* why you were so fed up!

I heard one of your mates talking to you. "Tough you didn't make the team, Dave." That's what he said.

I wonder what team?

Football? You certainly look fit.

They must be crazy not to pick you for this team. I'm not in any team either. But then I can't stand sports.

Sarah and I sometimes hide in the girls' toilets when it's Games.

But I can run fast.

I sometimes have to run like the wind when I get out of school to make sure I catch your bus.

I once saw you looking out of the window as I came running up to the bus stop.

Were you looking at me?

Love from
Katy
XXX

Dear Dave

Don't you like dancing?

Sarah said she was sure you'd be going to the Star Disco. You and your mates.

We went to the disco, Sarah and me.

I wore this new purple top. The exact purple of your school bag.

The purple top's a bit low cut for me. Sarah said it looked great but I wasn't sure. I didn't know what you'd think of it.

I so badly wanted you to think I looked great.

You'd ask me to dance and we'd be lit up in spangly lights.

Everyone would see us dancing together. Dave and Katy. A couple.

And then we'd go home together after the disco and we'd be in the dark but somehow the spangly lights would still be shining all round us.

That's the way I hoped it would be. But it didn't turn out like that.

You didn't turn up. Some of your mates were there. But you weren't.

Where were you on Friday night, Dave?

Have you got another girl?

I bet she doesn't care about you the way I do.

**Love from
Katy
XXX**

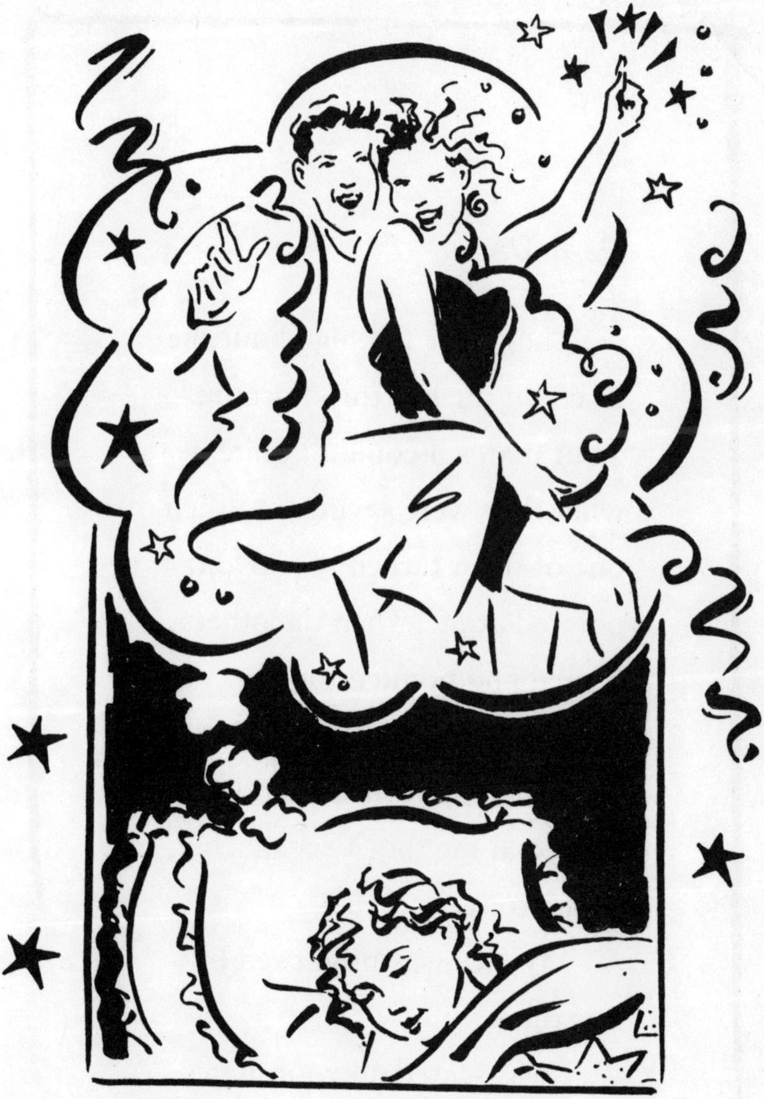

Dear Dave

They were talking about the disco on the bus this morning. Your mates. I couldn't quite hear what they were saying, but then one of them turned round and pointed at me. Then the others turned and pointed too.

I felt my face going pink.

Then you turned round and looked at me too. Very quickly, trying to seem casual.

My face was bright red by this time.

I was scared all your mates

were talking about my new purple top and saying I looked a right sight.

I was scared they were all laughing at me.

I was so so so scared you might laugh at me too.

But you didn't laugh. You just sort of smiled at me. You were a bit red in the face too.

Oh Dave, you've got such a lovely smile.

**Love from
Katy
xxx**

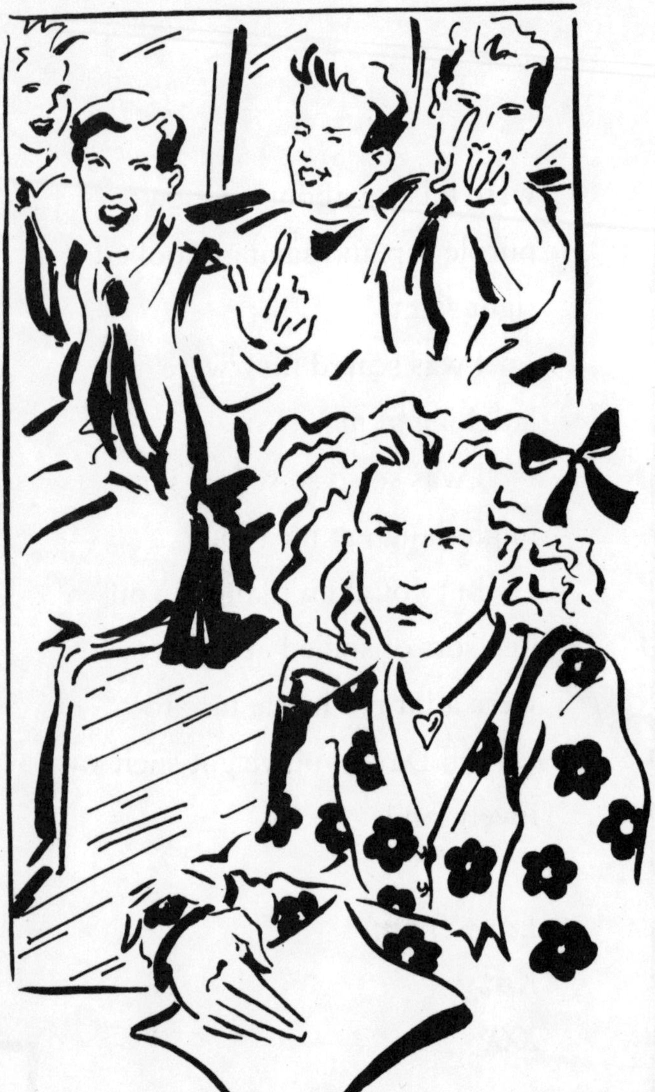

Dear Dave

You smiled at me on the bus again today.
I smiled back.
Oh Dave.

Love from
Katy
XXX

Dear Dave

Sarah says why don't I say something.

But I can't think what.

There's heaps and heaps and heaps I can write to you. But when I'm actually sitting right behind you on the bus I don't dare open my mouth.

I just smile.

When you smile at me.

Your mates all saw you smiling today. They all started teasing you.

"Who are you smiling at then, Dave? As if we didn't know!"

They kept on and on.

You told them all to shut up.

Then you gave me one last quick smile, like you were saying sorry.

It's OK, Dave. I understand. Truly I do.

Love from
Katy
XXX

Dear Dave

Maybe I don't understand. You came to the Star Disco this time. You and your mates.

My heart started thumping the moment I saw you. As if it was going to burst right out of my new purple top.

I went on dancing with Sarah, making out I hadn't seen you.

I went on and on dancing with Sarah.

You didn't come up to me.

You didn't ask me for a dance.

I waited the whole evening and you didn't even come near me.

You just hung about with all your mates.

I think you were looking at me though.

Don't you like my new purple top?

Don't you like me?

Oh Dave, what am I going to do?

**Love from
Katy
XXX**

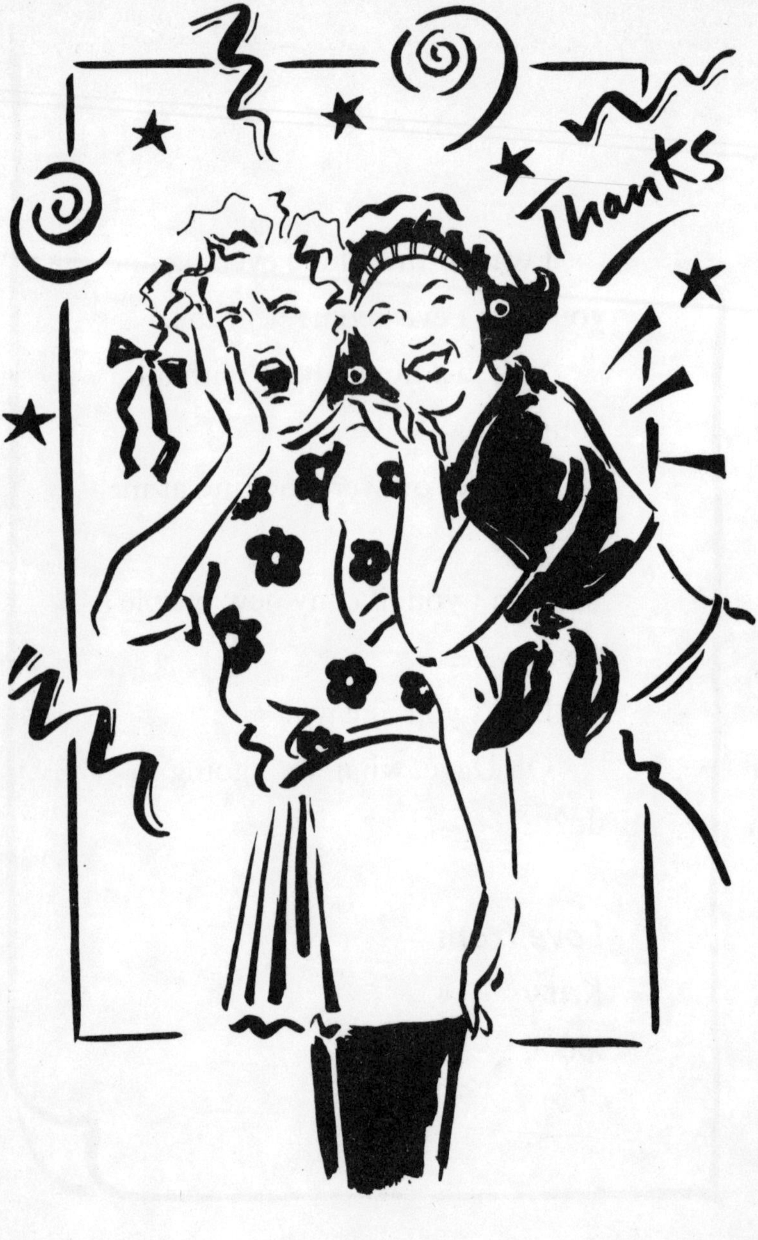
Thanks

Dear Dave

I am so fed up.

I'm sure you don't like me.

Even Sarah says maybe I'm wasting my time.

I gave her my new purple top. I couldn't stand the thought of ever wearing it again. It looks really good on her.

I don't think there's anything wrong with the top.

It's just me. Everything's wrong with me.

Oh Dave, if only you could make it all come right!

Love from
Katy
XXX

Dear Dave

I'm still fed up.

My mum's mad at me. She's found out I've given my purple top to Sarah.

My dad's mad at me. He says why do I have to go round looking miserable all the time.

He doesn't understand. Mum doesn't understand either. Sarah knows the way I feel about you. But even she doesn't understand.

I don't understand myself.

**Love from
Katy
XXX**

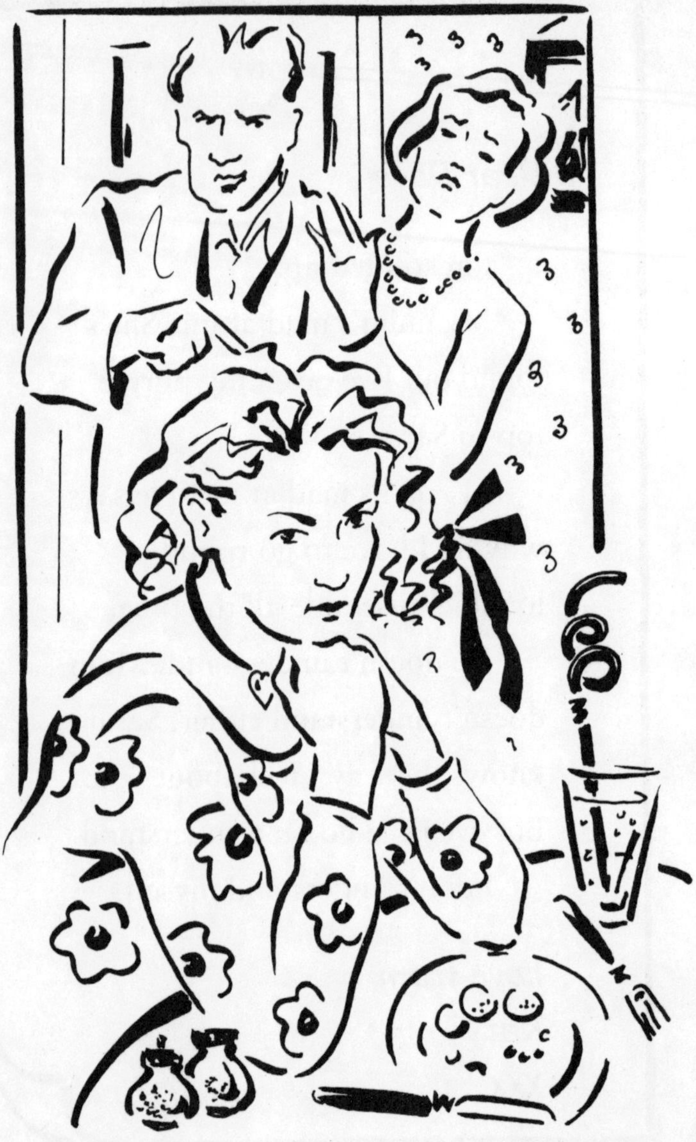

Dear Dave

I missed the bus this morning. I was late getting up.

I couldn't sleep properly for thinking about you. I think about you all the time.

I got into trouble at school. I was thinking about you instead of listening to the teacher.

"What's the matter with you, Katy?" she said. I just shrugged. I didn't want to tell her.

She thought I was being cheeky and she said I had to stay in after school.

So I missed the bus after school too.

Oh Dave, it's so awful not seeing you!

I miss you so very much.

**Love from
Katy
XXX**

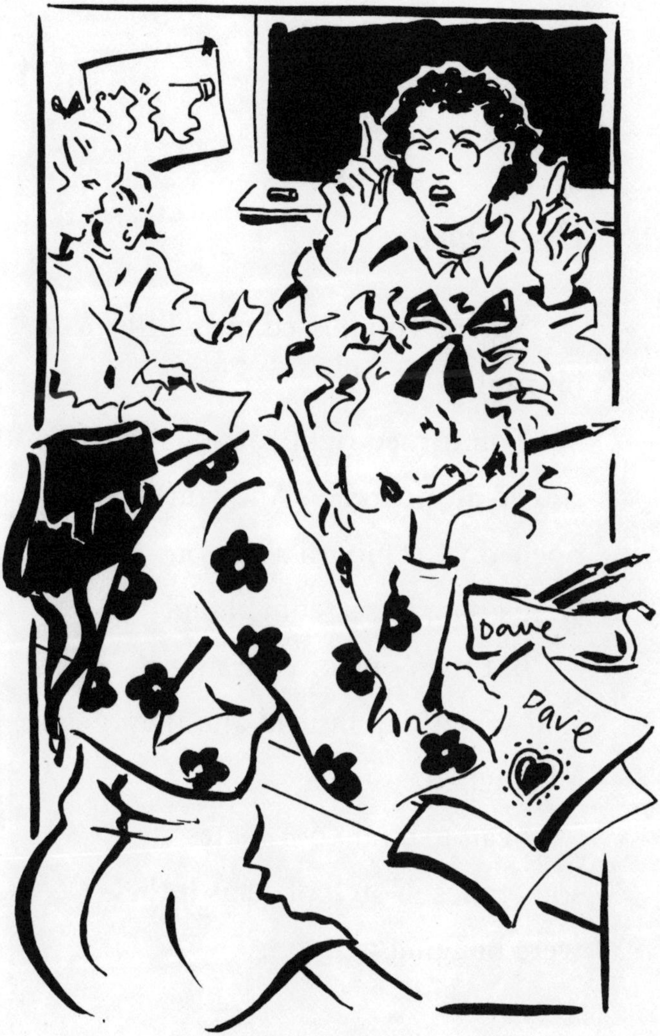
Dave
Dave

Dear Dave

Maybe you missed me a little bit too!

You turned right round and smiled at me today. And you opened your mouth as if you were going to say something.

But then one of your mates said something instead and they all laughed.

I can't stand your mates sometimes. You looked as if they were bugging you too.

If only we had the bus all to ourselves.

Just you and me.

Love from
Katy
XXX

Dear Dave

Oh no Oh no Oh no.

I saw you outside the fish and chip shop last night.

You were with your mates. And these two girls.

One of the girls looked very cute, with curly hair. She helped herself to your chips.

You didn't seem to mind. You smiled. At her.

Oh Dave, is she your girl?

Love from
Katy
XXX

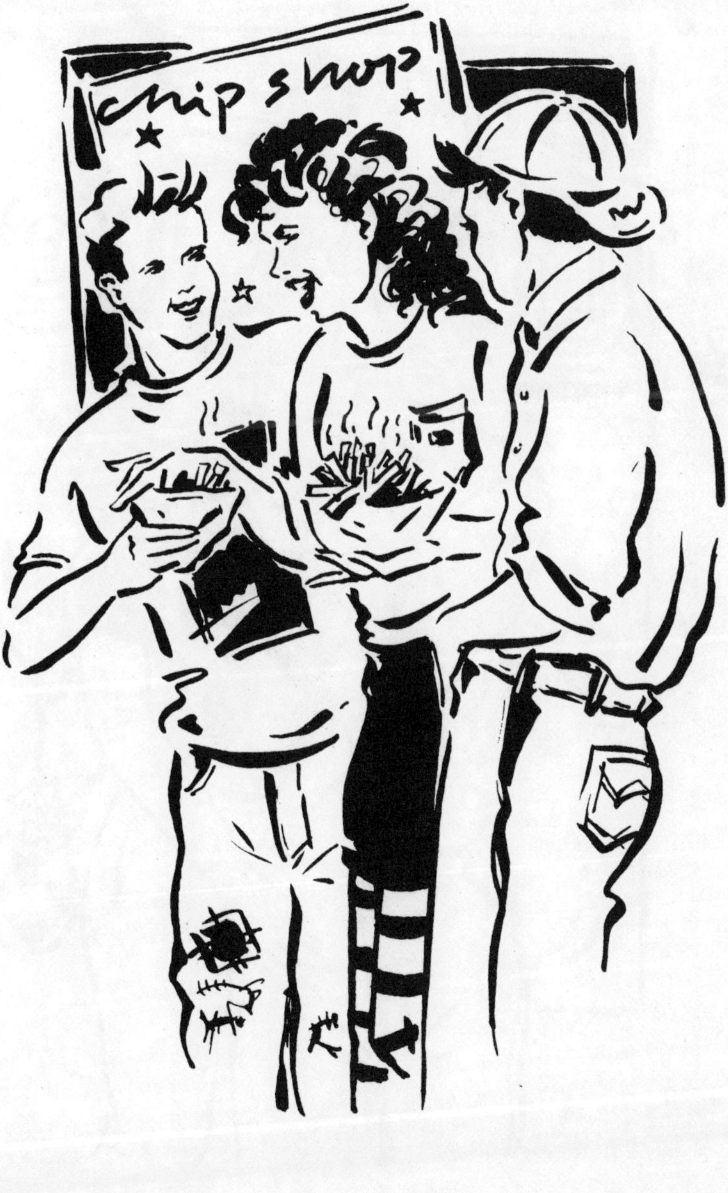
chip shop

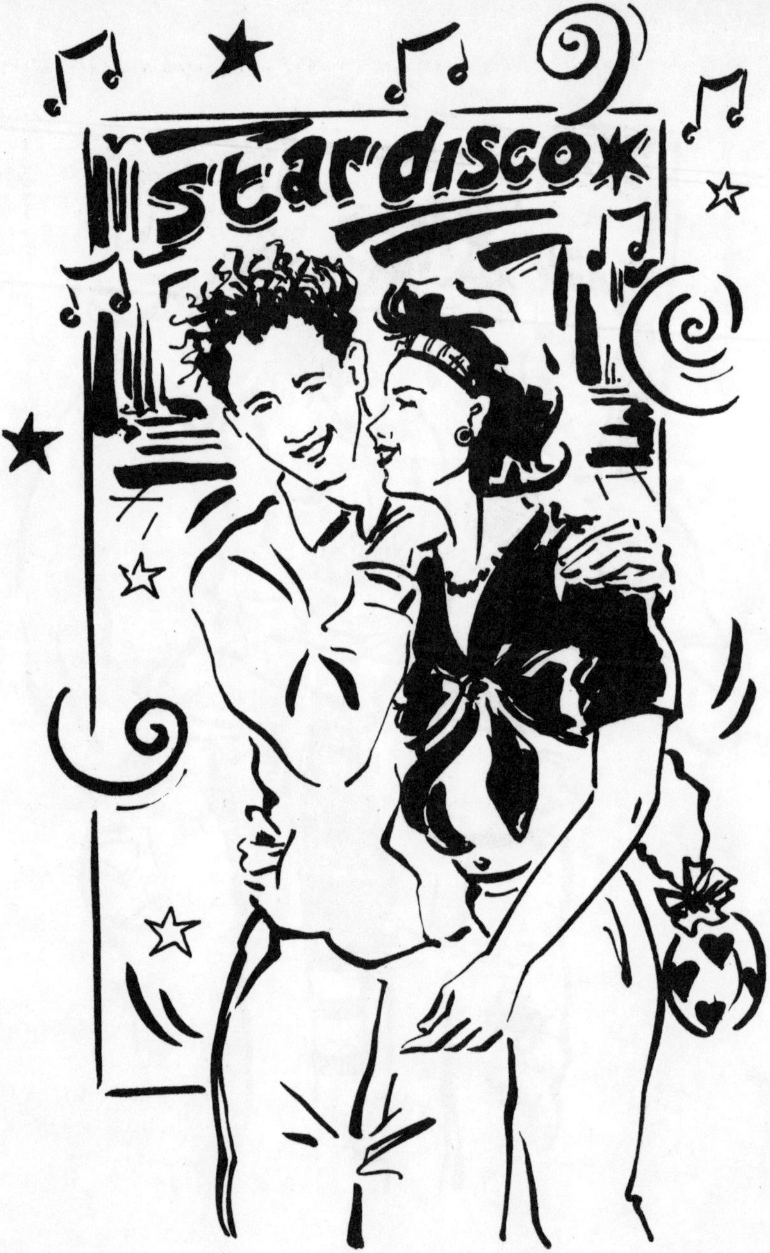
stardisco

Dear Dave

I told Sarah I wasn't going to the Star Disco again.

I said I couldn't bear the thought of seeing you there... with another girl.

Sarah wasn't at all understanding. She went to the disco with some other girls. She wore my new purple top.

She said this boy came up to her and said he thought she looked great. He said he particularly liked her purple top.

They danced together and then they had a drink together and then he walked her home.

I feel like Sarah has taken over my story as well as my purple top.

She went on and on about this boy. She got mad when I kept asking about you.

"Yes, Dave was there. I told you to go to the disco! What? No, I don't think he was with another girl."

She doesn't think.

She doesn't know for certain.

"Dave's the one who doesn't know anything," said Sarah. "Why don't you stop writing him all these dopey letters and just tell him you're nuts about him?"

Tell him.

Tell *you*.

Oh Dave.

I can't. I just can't.

**Love from
Katy
XXX**

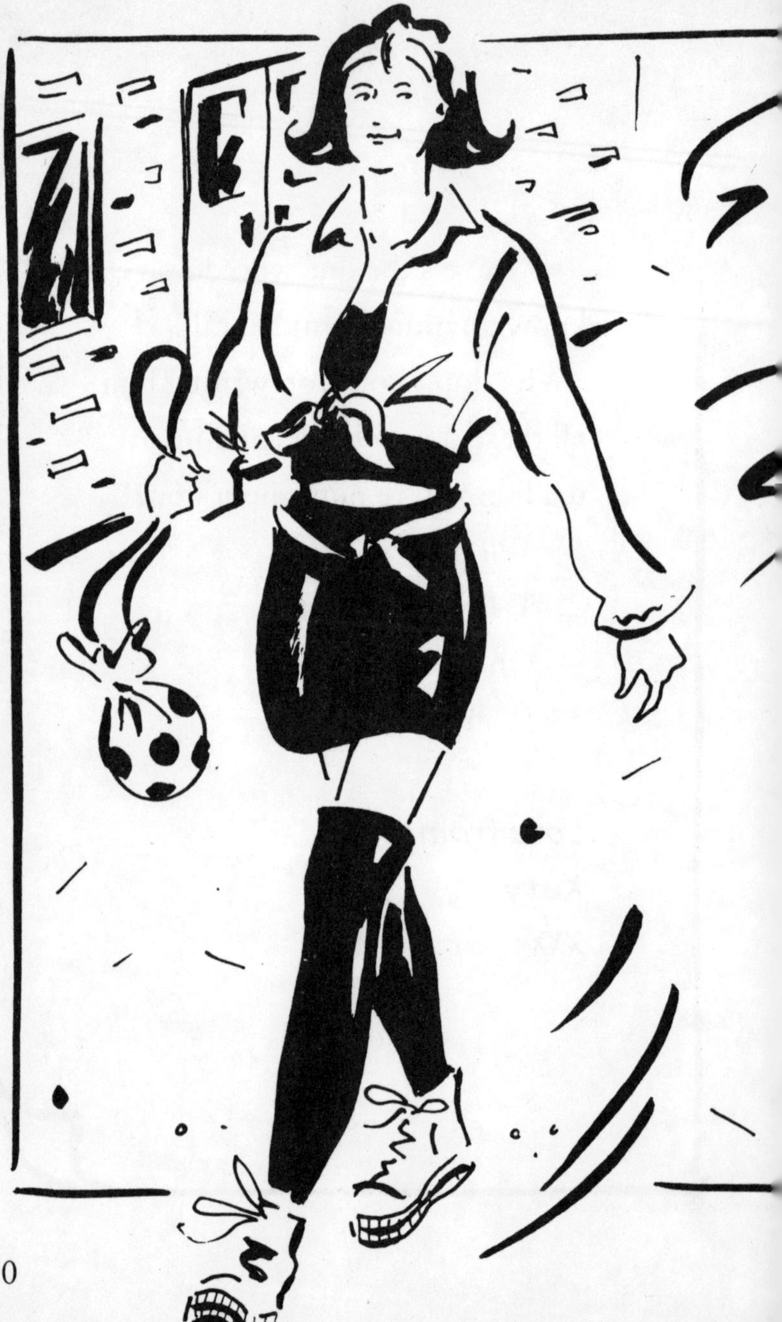

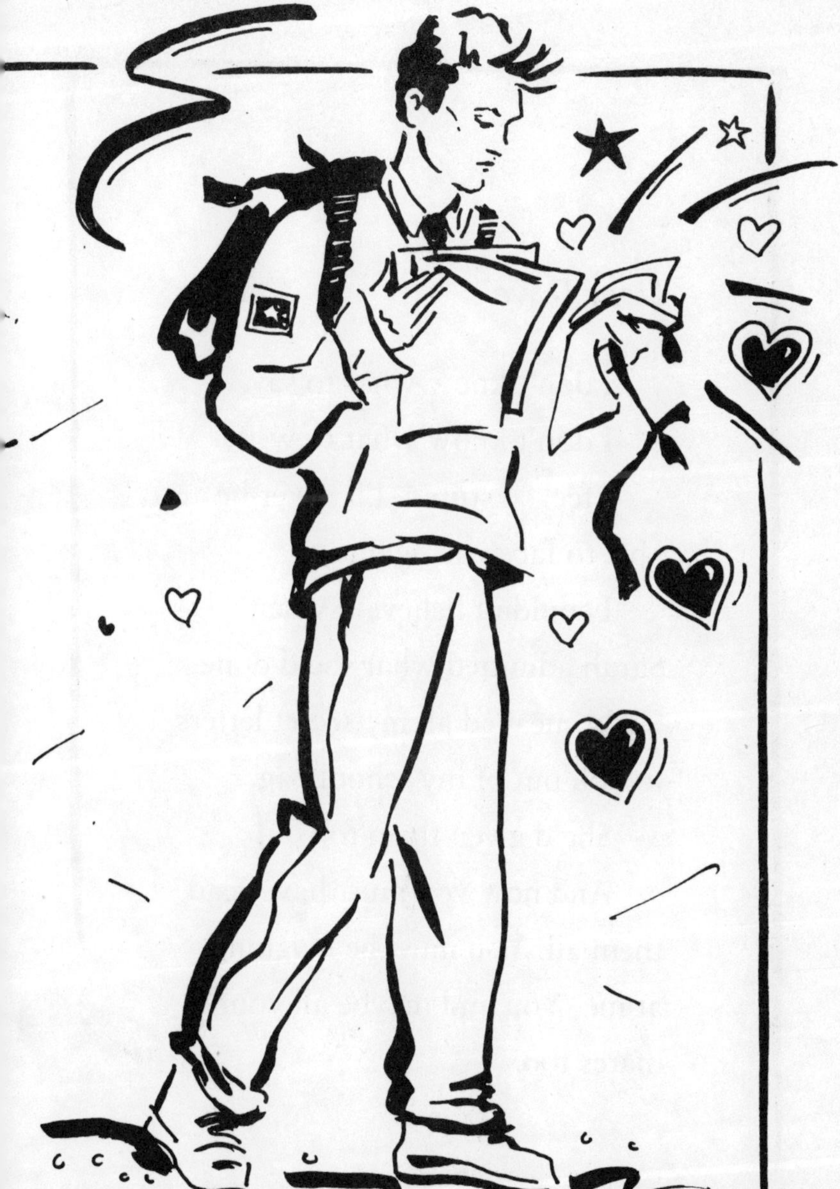

Dear Dave

I don't know what to say.

I don't know what to write.

I feel so stupid. I'll never be able to face you again.

I couldn't believe it when Sarah admitted what she'd done. She'd sneaked all my secret letters to you out of my school bag.

She'd given them to you!

And now you must have read them all. You must be laughing at me. You and maybe all your mates too.

I could kill Sarah, though she swears she was trying to do me a good turn.

I could kill *myself*.

I'm so sorry, Dave. I never meant anyone to read those letters but me.

This is the first letter that I shall really send to you.

It will be the last letter too.

Love from
Katy
XXX

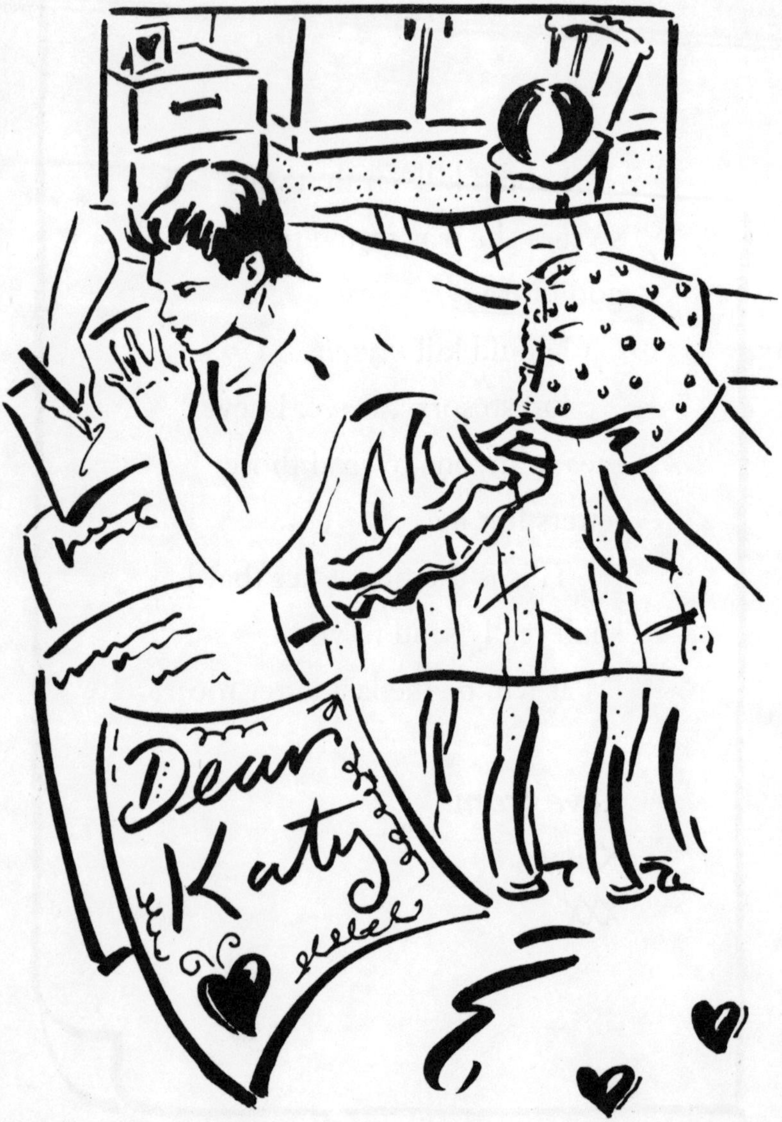
Dear Katy

Dear Katy

Please excuse this. I'm not much good at writing things down. I'm not much good at saying things either.

I've been wanting to say hello to you for ages. Ever since I first saw you on the bus.

I've been wanting to get to know you. But you know what it's been like, with all my mates. They don't half take the mickey.

My sister teases me too. She's the girl with the curly hair who stole my chips!

I didn't go to the Star Disco that first Friday because I was trying out for another team. (I made it this time!)

My mates said you were there. So I went next Friday.

I thought you looked really great. I wanted to dance with you. But I felt stupid in front of my mates. I'm not that great at dancing either, if you must know.

You're a truly fantastic dancer. I thought you'd maybe look down on me.

But it turns out you like me!
You've been writing me all these
secret letters. I couldn't believe it
when your mate Sarah gave them
to me.

At first I thought it was maybe
a joke.

But your letters aren't funny.
Your letters are lovely. The
loveliest letters in the whole world.

I think you're lovely too.
See you on the bus tomorrow!

Love from
Dave
XXXXX

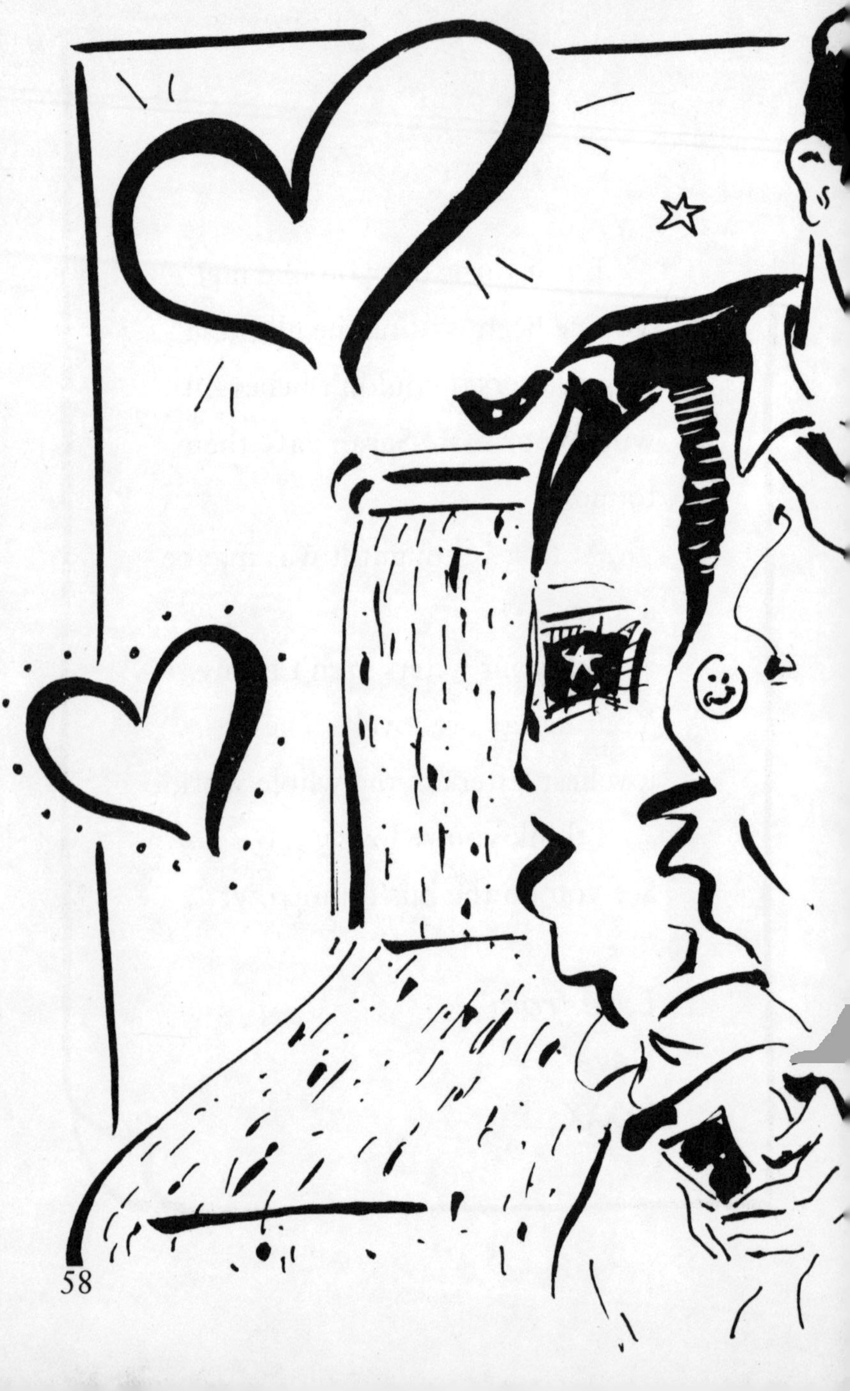

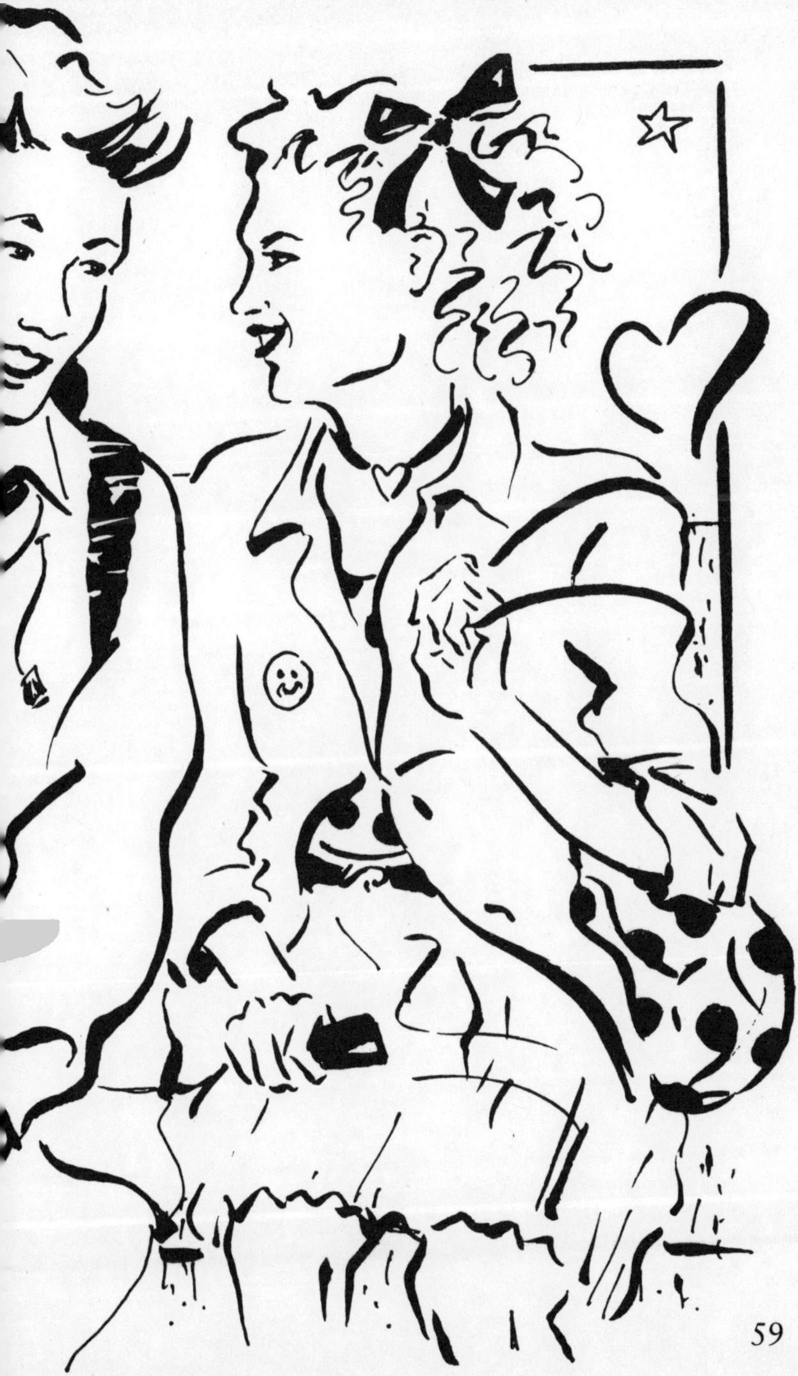

TEEN LIFE, SET C

Crush *by Jon Blake*

Ian's class have a wild time with their media studies project ... Somehow that video camera seems to land everyone in trouble – especially Ian!

Sweet Revenge *by Brian Caswell*

Nick's got a problem. He's being picked on by Budgie the bully – and he's had enough! He comes up with a plan to have a very sweet revenge.

Love from Katy *by Jacqueline Wilson*

Katy really likes Dave, a boy she's met on the bus. She doesn't dare tell him how she feels. So she writes letters instead – letters she never means to send. What would happen if Dave saw her letters?

ANOTHER BOOK BY JACQUELINE WILSON.

Sophie's Secret Diary

HUMOUR, SET B

Sophie's fed up with getting up at six to do her newspaper round. She's also fed up with not having a boyfriend. She's got her eye on someone – but does he have his eye on her?

IF YOU LIKED **LOVE FROM KATY**,
YOU MIGHT ENJOY ...

My Secret Love by Andy Brown

by Narinder Dhami

TEEN LIFE, SET D

"I've been in love now since 8.43 a.m. on January 14th, and it feels GREAT."

Andy loves Beth. But how can he tell her? Whenever he sees her, something's bound to go wrong ...